Introduction

Welcome to this new five-programme unit **Britons at War...** in the HOW WE USED TO LIVE series produced for Channel 4 Schools by Yorkshire International Thomson Multimedia Limited.

'Peace in Our Time' – was the hope of the British Prime Minister, Neville Chamberlain, and millions of people all over the world. This, as we know, was not to be: on September 3 1939, people clustered around their wireless sets to hear the news that the country was at war.

'**Britons at War**' vividly re-creates wartime Britain through a detailed, three-part drama, which follows the experiences of ten-year-old Jimmy in a period of traumatic change in British history.

Before the dramas a scene-setting documentary, **The Road to War**, charts the mood of the nation during the 1930's depression. The unit ends with the second documentary, **Never Again**, taking us from the end of the War in 1945 to the feel-good Festival of Britain in 1951. Both documentaries are richly interwoven with primary evidence.

This guide provides a wealth of ideas and stimulus for developing an exciting child-centred history based topic with many cross-curricular opportunities focusing on Britain since 1930.

Additional support is available through a poster of the period 1939–1945 and a resource pack which focuses on the effect of the War on everyday life in Britain, including food and rationing, clothes, transport and evacuation, War precautions.

We hope you enjoy the programmes. Please send any comments, suggestions or examples of children's work to the address below. They are always most welcome:

Rick Hayes
Education Officer
Channel 4 Schools
P O BOX 100
WARWICK
CV34 6TZ

CONTE

⟩ **Subtitles**
This **Channel 4 Schools** series is subtitled on Teletext for the deaf and hearing-impaired.

Using the programmes

Drama has a special place in the teaching of history. It offers a vivid picture of a past time which can be tested against other available evidence. The National Curriculum for England and Wales requires that children learn about the impact of the Second World War on everyday life. This unit of five programmes brings the period alive through a combination of drama and documentary and gives pupils access to complex issues through the medium of an exciting story.

It is a rich source of information which provides one version of the past. But there are others which children can use. Photographs and documents may tell a different story. The recollections of people who lived through the war vary tremendously depending on circumstances and by comparing real life memories with the experiences of characters in the dramas, children can begin to understand how and why interpretations of the past may differ.

Although history led, the programmes provide an opportunity to explore a range of related subjects, including science and technology, art, music and dance. Cross curricular links are identified on page 3.

Careful preparation ensures you get the most out of your viewing. Try to make time to:

- read through the programme notes and familiarise yourself with the background information;

- write a letter to parents and carers, describing the topic and appealing for contributions to a class museum.

- collect information books and pictures about World War II in general and life on the home front in particular.

- find out as much as possible about the impact of evacuation on your area.

Teachers' guide

This is designed to support your planning. It provides resources and ideas for preparation and follow-up but, as its name suggests, it is a guide, not a blueprint and it should be modified to meet the needs of your particular class.

The **background points** offer you, as a teacher information on historical events and developments which you may wish to discuss with the class.

Before viewing

Includes preparatory activities. It is important that children take an active part in viewing and one way to develop an enquiry approach is by briefing your class, before each programme, to look out for one particular theme or issue. Older children may wish to make brief notes on the chosen theme as they watch. Suggested topics are included for each programme.

Key vocabulary

This section alerts you to any unfamiliar words which you may wish to introduce before the programme begins.

While viewing

The use of a freeze-frame or pause facility is not recommended on the first showing of the programmes to pupils. However, such techniques are useful when re-viewing. Well chosen clips can be used to ask 'What do you think happens next?', to look at period details, to draw pupils' attention to particular events and to consider decisive moments at key points in the dramas.

Recap and consolidation

Enables you to check on literal recall and to unpack some of the more complex issues which are alluded to during the programmes. This can take the form of question and answer or discussion.

The impact of the war was felt in every town and village. Children need opportunities to relate what they have learned to their own local area and to find out how and why it was affected.

Ideas for developing the local perspective have been flagged in the Teacher's guide as

Local investigation

Use them to develop enquiry skills.

Activities suggested in the teachers' guide will help you to extend learning into a variety of subject areas. They are backed up by differentiated worksheets to support independent investigation. The first sheet for each programme is designed for the younger and less able pupil, while the second sheet is aimed at those who are ready for a greater challenge.

Further ideas for differentiation are included in the programme notes. Careful planning will help you to meet the needs of pupils across the ability range.

Before watching the series with the class, read the background information and then draw up a grid showing what you would expect pupils of differing abilities to know and understand by the end of the series.

Armed with this information, you can set precise learning targets for groups or individuals within your class.

Cross-curricular links

Programmes	Content	Cross-curricular links in the Teachers' Guide
1 The Road to War	■ Life in the 1930s ■ Technology in the 1930s ■ Hitler and the Jews	Using evidence – **His, Eng** Scrap book - **His, Eng, Art** Local investigation – **His, Geog, Eng** No electricity – **Sci, CDT** Ganging up – **PSE, Eng**
2 Nelson's Eye	■ Wartime London ■ Evacuation	Air raids and bomb shelters – **Sci, CDT** Living in the shelters – **PSE** Scrap book – **His, Eng, Art** Packing your suitcase – **PSE** Local investigation – **His, Geog** Evacuation role play – **His, Eng, Drama**
3 Run Rabbit, Run	■ Wartime in the country ■ Evacuation	Mapping the village – **Geog** Feeding Himmler – **IT** A wartime birthday party – **CDT** A postcard home – **Eng** Comic strip – **Art**
4 The Admiralty Regrets	■ The Blitz ■ Features of the war	Uniform for an air raid warden – **CDT** War work – **Eng, His** Shelter singsong – **Music** London night scene – **Art, English** Assessment sheet – **His**
5 Never Again	■ Building in the 1950s ■ Life in the 1950s ■ The Welfare State	After the war – **His, Geog** Changing town – **His, Geog** Scrap book – **His, Eng, Art** Class museum – **His, CDT** Health checks – **PSE, Sci**

The Road to War

Aims

In the years leading up to the Second World War, events in Britain and Germany ran in parallel. This documentary explores the experiences of both countries through the memories of three people who grew up in the 1930s.

Programme outline

Ken, Dorothy and Thea are in their seventies now. When they were children, war clouds were already gathering in Europe, but Ken and Dorothy, growing up in Britain remember secure childhoods. Dorothy lived with her family in a terrace house in Leeds. While she and her brother enjoyed swing bands and visits to the Saturday pictures, her parents were coming to grips with new technology in a time of rapid change. For Ken, who was eleven when war broke out, family life in the 1930s meant overcrowding and lack of privacy. He was already conscious of the gulf between the haves and have nots but, like many of his contemporaries, he saw the Nazis as figures of fun.

Meanwhile in Leipzig in Germany the memories of Thea Gersten, the daughter of a Jewish shopkeeper, are set against the backdrop of Hitler's rise to power. Her childhood ended one day in 1938 when her father's shop was smashed by Nazi supporters. The family fled to Poland, and there Thea's father remained while she and her mother escaped to Britain. She never saw him again. Hitler invaded Poland and Thea's father died in a concentration camp.

The programme ends with the declaration of war. The scene is set for the drama which follows.

Background points

Germany's economic troubles began with the massive reparations which she was forced to pay after losing World War I. She was already in difficulties when the Wall Street crash of 1929 triggered a world-wide depression. By the 1930s, the situation was desperate and the Germans were looking for a saviour and scapegoats. They found both through Hitler, a charismatic leader and a rabid anti-Semite who blamed the Jews for all Germany's problems. He promised to recover the territory lost after the First World War and to make the nation great again.

1933 Hitler becomes Chancellor of Germany

1936 German troops take back the Rhineland territories which were confiscated after World War I

March
1938 Germany and Austria merge
Nazis break up the shop belonging to Thea Gersten's father

September
1938 The Munich agreement – Germany invades Czechoslovakia

1939 Germany invades Poland
Britain declares war on Germany

Before viewing

Set the programme in time. Discuss periods previously studied and mark them on a time line. Add any other important events or periods which children may suggest. For younger children an approximate sequence is sufficient. Older pupils may be able to use precise dates to help them. When the class has suggested and sequenced about half a dozen times from history introduce the period covered by this programme and add it to the time line.

Look at a map of Europe and locate Great Britain, Germany and Poland.

Find out what, if anything, children already know about Hitler and the Nazi treatment of the Jews.

The three contributors present different versions of events. Brief children to look out for:

- similarities and differences in their stories;

- contrasts between life in Britain and Nazi Germany.

Key words

terrace house, wireless, dictator, politicians, concentration camp, bolster, cooking range, taper, flat iron, Gypsies (now often called travellers), Nazis, Adolf Hitler, Jews, Bren gun

After viewing
Recap and consolidation

- How was life in 1930s Britain different from that today? What are the points of similarity?

- How do Ken and Dorothy's recollections differ?

It is important to explore the ethical issues raised by Thea's story but the approach will depend very much on pupils' age, understanding and background. Not all primary aged children will be ready to absorb the full implications of the Holocaust and the programme's treatment of references to Hitler's policies leaves teachers free to follow up in the way best suited to their particular class.

Memories of the past

Activity sheet 1 (page 6)

This questionnaire which is appropriate for younger or less able pupils can be used either in the classroom or as a homework exercise to structure an interview with a person in his or her 70s. The headings match the topics covered by Ken and Dorothy and children should be encouraged to look for differences and similarities in the recollections of people interviewed.

Older children can undertake the same activity but they could be expected to devise their own interview sheet, using the published one as a model if inspiration flags.

Using evidence

Activity sheet 2 (page 7)

Activities like this help children to understand how we find out about the past. The book based research could be undertaken in class, and followed up at home by discussion with older people. Younger children could confine their researches to one event. Older and abler pupils should be encouraged to complete the whole sheet and, as an extension, to present their findings as a display.

Scrap book

Start a Britain since 1930s scrap book, in three sections – before the war, wartime itself, and post war. Concentrate on the pre-war section and collect details of people's memories, family photographs, examples of magazines, postcards, stamps, etc to be photocopied and pasted in the scrap book.

🔍 Local investigation

History around us

Researching the local area helps children to relate the period they are studying to their own lives. Useful sources for a local investigation include:

Old photographs There may be a published collection for your area. Alternatively, try your nearest public library or record office.

Oral history Local history societies often have documented oral histories and children can read, or be read extracts of these.

School log books These can give useful insights into school life in the period.

Newspapers Reference libraries may hold old newspapers on microfilm. Compare a copy of a local newspaper from the period with today's equivalent.

No electricity

By the 1930s, Dorothy's terraced house had electricity, but Ken and his family had to manage without. If you can, get hold of some household artefacts from the 1930s and talk about alternatives to electric power.

	Ken's house	Dorothy's house
Lighting		
Cooking		
Heating		
Ironing		
Bathing		

Ganging up

Why do people discriminate against other people? What should we do about it? Ask children for examples of 'ganging up'. Talk about occasions in the past when they, or you, have felt left out. This could be developed, through small group discussion, into individual role play. Children should be encouraged to reflect on their experiences in writing or through pictures, music or dance.

Memories of the past

Talk to somebody in their seventies. Ask them what they remember about their childhood.

This is what .... remembers

Having a bath

Keeping warm in bed

Cooking and kitchens

Telephones

School

Entertainments

Does the person you interviewed remember the same things as Dorothy and Ken?

What differences can you spot?

Why do you think people remember the past in different ways.

How We Used to Live Britons at War

Using evidence

We can learn about the past from books, from television programmes and from the memories of people who lived then. They are all **sources** of information.

Find out more about these people and events from books, and from older people.

The day war broke out

Adolf Hitler

The first telephones

The Nazis

Germany's invasion of Poland

Sir Winston Churchill

The Jarrow March

Walt Disney and films of the 1930s

Which source of information told you most? Put a ring round the one which was most helpful.

books   **television**   **people's memories**

How We Used to Live Britons at War

Nelson's Eye

Aims

This programme, which is the first of three linked dramas, explores the experiences of city children during the Blitz.

Programme outline

It is March 1941 in the East End of London and the Blitz is at its height. Jimmy and Barbara Tyler with their mother Ida, spend their nights sheltering in the underground with Miriam Rosenthal, an Austrian Jewish refugee who runs the corner shop with her husband Manny and son Simon (Simey to his friends).

Their father is at sea, serving on the HMS Hood. While Ida works as a 'nippy' at the Lyons Corner House, Grandad Tyler, an ex-sailor with a glass eye cheers Jimmy with stories of great naval battles, and Barbara dreams of living like a lady in a big house in the country.

Jimmy gets involved with the local spiv and learns about the Rosenthals' flight from Nazi Austria. When the air raid siren sounds, he cannot be found. His home is destroyed by a bomb, and, although Barbara escapes unhurt, Grandad is killed. London is too dangerous for the children and Ida and the other parents reluctantly agree to evacuate their children. Barbara and Jimmy and their friends are to be sent to the country. The programme ends with their departure.

Background points

The first evacuations began as soon as war broke out. The whole country was divided into evacuation, reception and neutral areas. Thousands of school age children were sent from evacuation to reception areas for safety. But many drifted back to the cities during the first year when the expected air raids failed to materialise.

In August 1940 the Battle of Britain began as the Luftwaffe attempted to destroy RAF air fields in preparation for an invasion. When this failed, the Luftwaffe changed tactics and bombed major cities. The East End of London suffered particularly badly from nightly attacks on the docks. During the Blitz many Londoners took refuge in communal shelters or in the tunnels of the underground.

During the raids, volunteers such as 'Skidlid' the special constable, and Stanley patrolled the streets. ARP stands for Air Raids Protection and it was Stanley's job to enforce blackout regulations. He was in charge of shelters and had to keep a look-out during air raids.

Meanwhile merchant ships faced a dangerous passage through enemy waters. They were organised into convoys, guarded by Royal Naval battleships, such as HMS Hood. But one in four was sunk and shortages resulted in rationing and the kind of black market trading which Stanley undertook.

Before viewing

Prepare the children to look out for:

- signs of the Blitz, including bomb damage and different kinds of precautions
- different kinds of uniform
- gas masks

Key words

Blitz, raids, evacuation, munitions, spiv, black market, Nelson, invincible, nippy (waitress), baccy (tobacco), Sabbath

After viewing

Recap and consolidation

- How was everyday life affected by the bombing? Which aspects of life remained the same, and which were changed?
- What was Stanley selling? Why did people buy nylons and chocolate from him, rather than from a shop? Why did Grandad condemn black marketeers?
- Draw out links between the fictional experiences of the characters in this episode and those of the real characters interviewed for the first programme.
- Talk about the Rosenthals' Sabbath supper. If possible, invite a member of the Jewish community to talk to the children about Jewish beliefs and traditions.

Air raid and bomb shelters

How did people protect themselves during the air raids? Get children to find out about different kinds of shelter including communal shelters, Anderson shelters and Morrison shelters.

The Anderson shelter was designed for householders with gardens. The Morrison shelter, which came later, could be erected indoors.

Which are the best materials for building an air raid shelter? What is the best shape for the roof?

Living in the shelters

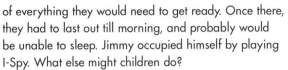

At bedtime city children learned to leave their clothes out ready for a night-time dash to shelter. Get the class to make a list of of everything they would need to get ready. Once there, they had to last out till morning, and probably would be unable to sleep. Jimmy occupied himself by playing I-Spy. What else might children do?

Scrap book

Extend the scrap book by developing a section on life in wartime. This might include copies of photographs, postcards, documentation, newspaper clippings about the area and memories of older people. When gathering this evidence, relate it to that seen in the television programme, highlighting differences as well as similarities. This helps children to understand the diversity of wartime experiences.

Packing your suitcase

Activity sheet 3 (page 10)

> **Clothing and documents required:**
> - sandwiches
> - gas mask
> - a change of underclothes
> - night clothes
> - house shoes or plimsolls (daps)
> - spare stockings or socks
> - a toothbrush
> - comb
> - towel
> - a coat
> - boots
> - ration book, identity card

🔍 Local investigation

Evacuation areas

Activity sheet 4

Find out from your local Records Office or large library whether your school was in an evacuation, reception, or neutral area. Look for clues to what happened in the past. Are there any traces of a wartime airfield in the locality? Are there signs of rebuilding in an old city centre or church records of bomb deaths. In reception areas, the school log may recall details of the arrival of evacuees. Ask local people about their memories of the war and look through wartime editions of the local paper. Interesting sections can be photocopied for use in the classroom.

Evacuation role play

Activity sheets 3, 4 and 13 could be used as part of an evacuation day role play as follows:

Children arrive at the assembly point (the school hall) in coats and thick shoes, carrying luggage, packed lunch and gas mask box. They are checked off on a register. Children might adopt role names for the occasion.

Adults, in role, check that each child has brought a ration book, identity card and gas mask, and that they have a suitable packed lunch.

Children complete luggage labels and are issued with postcards before, waved off by weeping mothers, they head for the railway station, or another suitable gathering point. If possible, liaise with another school to role play arrival in the reception area.

Evacuation poems

Encourage the children to explore the feelings of an evacuee through poetry. Here is an example written by a 10-year-old from Coventry.

Evacuee

Children in a long line
Faces all the same
Inside themselves, confused and angry
On their coats, their name
Mothers weeping
Children cry
As they part and say goodbye
As the train moves out of the station
Children wave goodbye
Then sitting back in his chair
A boy lets out a sigh
When they reach their destination
The train chuffs into the noisy station
The children make their way to the village hall
The children are all different sizes
Some skinny, some short, some tall
When they arrive, they march around
Most looking at feet or ground
When at last, most have been claimed
There is just the boy
Pale and bedraggled the boy clasps a precious toy
The boy feel sad and alone
As a man takes him to the office
He doesn't know where he's going to go...

Jenny Roper (10)
Mount Nod Primary School

Packing your suitcase

Imagine you are being evacuated. You can take a suitcase with you containing a set of clothes. These, the clothes you are wearing, and a few things which you can see around the suitcase are all you will have.

▶ Draw the clothes you have chosen in the suitcase on a separate sheet. Explain why you have chosen them.

▶ Draw any other belongings, such as a toothbrush, which you must have.

▶ Now choose three special things to take with you.

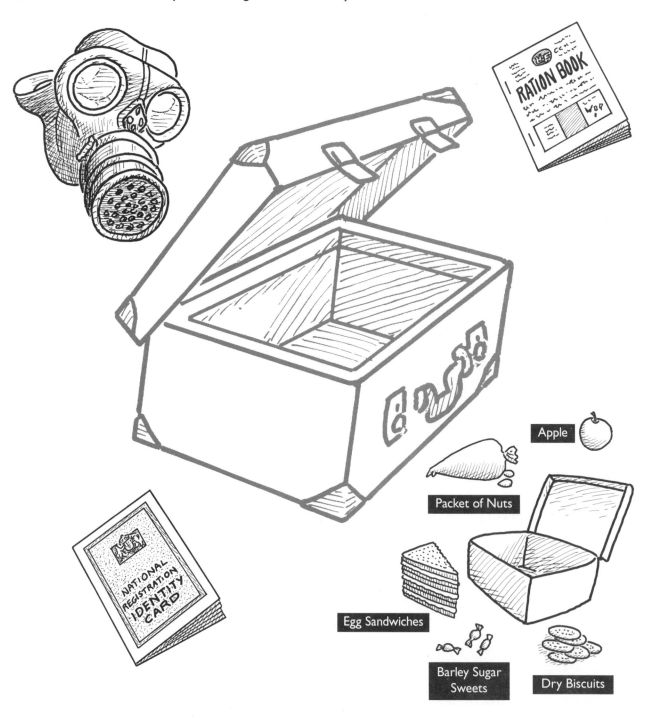

RATION BOOK

Apple

Packet of Nuts

NATIONAL REGISTRATION IDENTITY CARD

Egg Sandwiches

Barley Sugar Sweets

Dry Biscuits

How We Used to Live Britons at War

4 SCHOOLS

Evacuation areas

Children were evacuated from the cities to escape the bombing.

What happened in your area?

Look on the map and find:

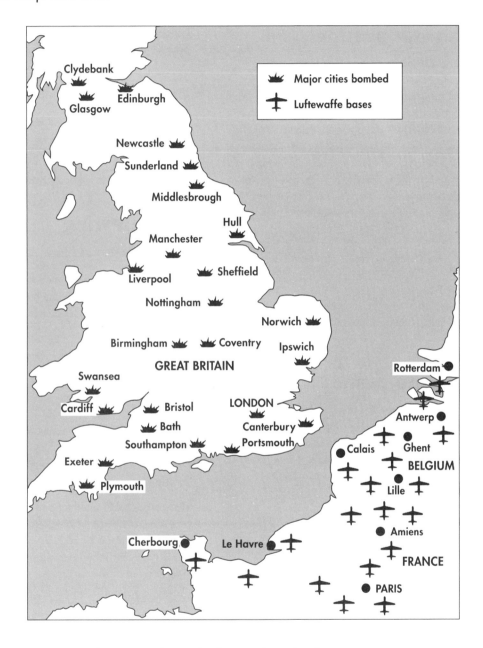

▶ The nearest city to where you live which was bombed.

▶ Try to find out what happened to schools in your area.

▶ Which parts of Great Britain suffered most from the bombing?

▶ Which suffered least?

▶ Think of some reasons why.

How We Used to Live Britons at War

3 Run Rabbit, Run

Aim

This programme, which is the second of three linked dramas, looks at the impact of the war upon country life and explores the experience of evacuation.

Programme outline

Jimmy, Barbara and the other evacuees from Nelson Street get off the train at the north country village of Moorside and are claimed by the waiting villagers. Barbara is carried off to the big house to be a companion for the doctor's daughter, Marianne. Jimmy, with Simey and Marty end up at Overblow, the bleak hill farm belonging to Piggy Dent and his wife Norah. Hard work, grim conditions and the hostility of pupils at the village school make them long to return to London. A pig killing is the last straw and they decide to run away.

Meanwhile Barbara is finding that her dreams of grandeur are not matched by reality. Marianne is snobbish and resentful of Barbara's presence. Finally, unable to bear Marianne's taunting any longer, Barbara empties a bowl of trifle over her head at a birthday tea and joins the Nelson Street group on their flight to London.

Background points

In the towns a local government official was usually given the job of billeting officer. In rural areas a volunteer was appointed to supervise the procedure. Mrs Green, the doctor's wife is a typical choice. Billeting was compulsory and anyone who refused to take in an evacuee could be fined.

The allowance of 10s 6d (52.5p) for the first evacuee and 8s 6d (42.5p) for each additional child was intended to cover living costs. All but the poorest parents were expected to pay about two-thirds of this while the government made up the shortfall. Many families found it hard to keep up the payments and reclaimed their children.

Farming played an important part in the war effort and was closely regulated. Animal food was rationed and farmers had to account for all beasts slaughtered. Nevertheless opportunities for black market dealings existed and were exploited by many farmers, such as Piggy Dent.

Before viewing

Prepare the children to look out for:

- signs of war in the countryside, to be compared with those in the cities. For example, home guards drilling, name of the railway painted out, cow painted with white stripes to make it visible during the blackout;

- differences between life in the doctor's house and at Piggy Dent's farm;

- similarities between the way of life remembered by Ken and Dorothy in programme 1, and that experienced by Jimmy and Barbara in this programme.

Key words

Himmler (SS Chief Heinrich Himmler), Eva Braun (Adolf Hitler's mistress), rationing, billeting officer, cockneys, 'Japs' (Japanese), HMS Hood, Battle of Trafalgar

After viewing

Recap and consolidation

- Why were children evacuated from the cities? Was it a good idea or not? Was the homesickness and discomfort worth it to keep children safe from bombing?

- Talk about the children's feelings as they waited to be picked. This could be used as the basis for a role play, with one or two children hot-seated afterwards to describe their emotions.

- What differences did children notice between war time in the city and the country? How were the people of Moorside preparing for a possible invasion?

- The story is told from the point of view of the visiting evacuees, but what was the reaction of the village children? Arrange for children from another class to share your classroom and resources for the morning. What sort of problems arise?

- Were Jimmy and his friends right to return to London? Were they justified in stealing the farmer's truck?

A postcard home

Activity sheet 5 (page 14)

Before undertaking this exercise, children should have an opportunity to compare the experiences shown in the programme with others, both in real life and in fiction in order to develop their understanding of the diverse reactions to evacuation. If possible, invite into the classroom people who were evacuated during the war and talk to them about what they remembered.

Failing that, Robert Westall's non-fiction anthology, *Children of the Blitz* (ISBN 0006750869), is a superb teaching resource. A wide range of men and women from all over Britain remember what it was like to grow up in wartime. The book consists of short, vivid snippets arranged by subject and that on evacuation is particularly strong.

Extracts from works of fiction such as *Goodnight Mr Tom* (ISBN 0140372334) by Michelle Magorian could be used to broaden children's experience and to drive home the all important point that although evacuation was a common experience, reactions to it were as individual as the people who took part.

Cartoon story

Activity sheet 6 (page 15)

The Giles cartoon shows yet another, comic version of evacuees. Older and abler children should be encouraged to evaluate it as evidence. How useful is it? What does it tell us about people's attitudes?

Extracts from Richmal Crompton's *William and the Evacuees* (ISBN 0333436741) provide a good comparison.

A blank comic strip is available on page 26.

Mapping the village

Ask children to name the different features of the village of Moorside and to draw them on a sketch map. Label the billets of the different characters. Compare the sketch map with an OS map of a real village. How does the real village differ from the fictional one?

- Overblow Farm
- Dr and Mrs Green's house.
- The pub
- Village school
- Railway station
- Potato fields
- Vicar's house

This could be developed into a display by adding pictures of the different evacuees together with captions or extended writing about their experiences in the country.

Feeding Himmler

Marty, Simey and Jimmy were warned to keep out of Himmler's way, but from time to time it was necessary to enter his sty, and then he was held at bay with a pitchfork.

Nowadays we could use control technology to solve the problem. Get your class to design a pigsty with a separate enclosure which can be barred or unbarred by remote control once Himmler is inside it.

Use a program such as Control Logo/Contact and a buffer box to design and build a system which will keep the evacuees safe when they enter Himmler's enclosure.

A wartime birthday party

By 1941 rationing was in full swing and there were many shortages. Lack of ingredients made it impossible to produce a proper birthday cake and some families used a cardboard one instead. This was the menu for one typical wartime party.

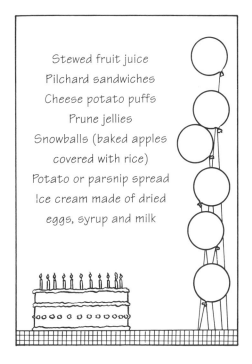

Stewed fruit juice
Pilchard sandwiches
Cheese potato puffs
Prune jellies
Snowballs (baked apples covered with rice)
Potato or parsnip spread
Ice cream made of dried eggs, syrup and milk

Try this wartime recipe

Mock marzipan potatoes

Ingredients;

1 oz margarine
2 tablespoons water
2 – 3 teaspoons almond essence
4 oz sugar
4 oz dried haricot beans
Cocoa powder

Soak haricot beans overnight, then boil for one hour.

Mash well with a fork.

Add the other ingredients and break into small pieces, about the size of a new potato.

Shape and roll in cocoa powder.

A postcard home

Imagine you are one of the characters from the programme. Write a postcard or a letter home, describing your first day in Moorside.

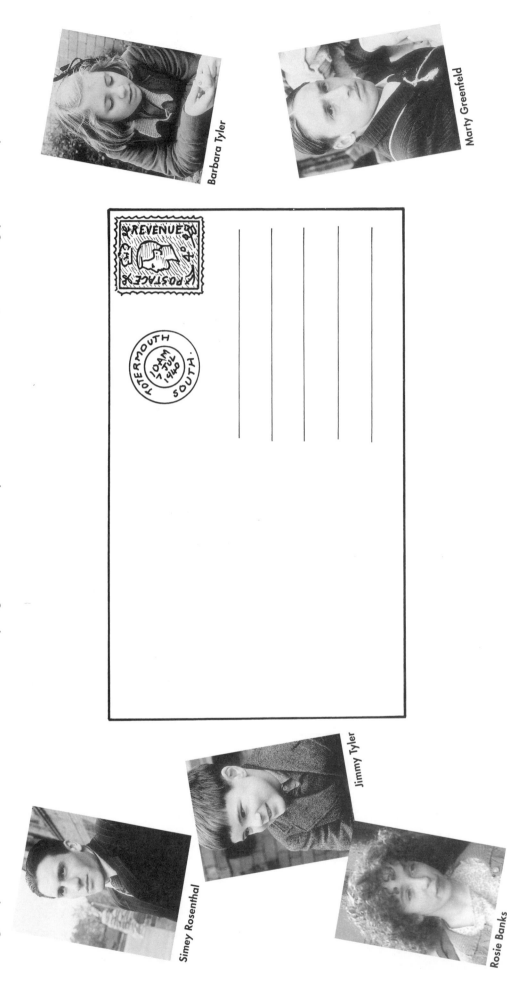

Barbara Tyler

Marty Greenfeld

Simey Rosenthal

Jimmy Tyler

Rosie Banks

Show what you have written to one of your friends. See if your friend can guess which of the evacuees wrote the letter.

Points of view

How many evacuees can you
see in the picture?

What are they all doing?

What do you think the owner of
the house and his gardener are
saying to each other?

"If this new attack on the Western Front means the end of the war, I suppose we shall be losing our little evacuee friends, your lordship."

Sunday Express, Mar. 4th, 1945

How We Used to Live Britons at War

The Admiralty Regrets

Aims

This programme places the events of the Blitz and evacuation within the wider context of the war in Europe and at sea.

Programme outline

Jimmy, Barbara and their friends have escaped from Moorside in Piggy Dent's van but it breaks down and the evacuees are stranded in the countryside and pursued by a heavily camouflaged detachment of the Home Guard.

It is dark when they reach London and the raids have already begun. They find the corner shop closed and the Rosenthals gone. Skidlid, the unpopular special constable has reported them to the authorities as enemy aliens and they have been interned. Ida knows what has happened to them, but she is missing too, and the munitions factory where she worked has suffered a direct hit.

Desperate for news, they make their way through the deserted streets to the Underground where they find her sheltering with workmates from the munitions factory.

But, though the Rosenthals are safe, another danger looms. News comes through that the German battleship, the Bismarck has sunk the HMS Hood and there are no survivors. The street is in mourning for Alf Tyler but, just as Jimmy is giving up hope and smashes 'Nelson's Eye' against a wall, he sees his father approaching. An injury kept him on shore when the Hood sailed and he was saved from the disaster. The story ends on a sombre note as Alf tells the story of the destruction of a mighty battleship and the death of his shipmates. But the family is reunited, however briefly, and the sun is shining. Despite the destruction there is hope.

Background points

The Home Guard was a voluntary body of men who, either because of their age or occupation were excluded from active service with the armed forces. Their task was to defend the countryside against invasion.

Enemy aliens, a category which included German and Austrian refugees, were identified and registered at the beginning of the war but those classified as low risk were left in peace until May 1940 when they were rounded up and interned on the orders of the Home Secretary John Anderson. Most ended up in the Isle of Man and were gradually released as the war proceeded.

The Bismarck, which sank the British battle cruiser HMS Hood was herself scuttled during her next encounter with the British fleet. The result was acclaimed as a great victory and news of it was flashed around the world.

Before viewing

Prepare the children to look out for:

- patches of white paint intended to help people to dodge obstacles in the blackout;

- sandbagged buildings;

- temporary notices showing the impact of the war on everyday life.

Key words

internment, All Clear, the Bismarck, ghetto, nark (informer), Greenland, Scapa Flow

After viewing

Recap and consolidation

- What had happened to the Rosenthals? Why were they interned?

- Think about some of the opinions of Jews expressed by characters in the dramas. How did attitudes in wartime Britain compare with those in Nazi Germany? How fair were the judgements expressed?

- Why were Stanley and Skidlid out during the air raid. What were their duties? What dangers might they face?

Uniform for an air raid warden

Activity sheet 7 (page 18)

Most men and women were in some kind of government directed work, and the majority wore uniforms. Get children to think about those they have seen in the dramas. They include special constable, Home Guard, soldier, sailor, nippy, munitions worker, land girl, and RAF officer. Compare them with photographs from the period before designing an outfit for Stanley.

War work

Activity sheet 8 (page 19)

Although many women joined the services, their role was to support the front line fighters and they did not see action. But on the home front women served as fire watchers and air raid wardens. They drove ambulances and worked in canteens in the blitz, and policed the cities as special constables.

Women were encouraged to take over men's jobs during the war. For many it was a first taste of independence, which they were reluctant to relinquish when the war was over.

Shelter singsong

The nights in the shelters were long and uncomfortable. Some Londoners kept their spirits up by singing. Popular songs included Run Rabbit, Run, The Quartermaster's Stores, Roll Out the Barrel, I'm Going to Hang My Washing on the Siegfried Line, Hands, Knees and Bumpsa Daisy and She'll be Coming Round the Mountain. Children could make up their own actions for the last two. Words for The Quartermasters' Stores can be found on page 25.

> *Run rabbit, run rabbit*
> *Run, run, run*
> *Run rabbit, run rabbit*
> *run, run, run,*
> *Bang, bang, bang, bang*
> *goes the farmer's gun*
> *Run rabbit, run rabbit*
> *Run, run, run.*

London night scene

Ask children to select their own media to make a picture of an air raid, drawing on scenes from the drama, and the memories of eye witnesses.

"*The sky over London was glorious, as though a dozen suns were setting...Everywhere the shells sparkled like Christmas baubles.*"

"*The raiders would drop parachute flares, magnificent fireworks which drifted slowly down.*"

"*Suddenly a street would be carpeted with brilliant incendiaries, hissing and sparkling with a whitish green glare.*"
(Angus Calder, The People's War)

Reprinted by kind permission of The Peters, Fraser and Dunlop Group Ltd.

This could be linked to descriptive writing, or poetry about an air raid.

Assessment sheet (page 24)

This tests children's knowledge and understanding about key features of life in wartime. When children have completed the first section, discuss the features they have come up with and produce a class list. Make sure it includes:

- bombing, blackout, evacuation, shelters

- war at sea, rationing, make do and mend, dig for Victory

- invasion, Home Guard, taking down sign posts, identity cards.

Level 1/2 Can identify two or three obvious features which relate to everyday life, for example, bombing, evacuation. Little attempt at linking key features.

Level 3 Shows some evidence of a wider context. May mention one of the following: fear of invasion, war at sea, experiences in Germany. Can make simple links, for example, blackout/bombing.

Level 4/5 Several of the key features mentioned relate to the wider context. Makes clear links between different key features. Can explain how the war at sea, on land and in the air affected everyday life.

Uniform for an air raid warden

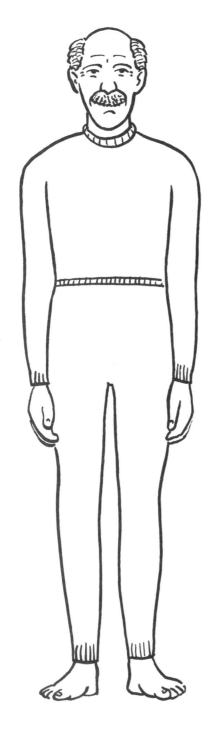

DUTIES OF AN AIR RAID WARDEN

Check that all houses are blacked out
Find out which houses are empty
Know where everyone is during the raid
Keep people in shelters calm
Keep a look out during raids
Watch out for looters

Stanley has to stay up all night when the bombs are falling.

Design him a uniform which will keep him warm and safe.

What other pieces of equipment does he need?

What will he do about food and drink?

How We Used to Live Britons at War

4 SCHOOLS

War work

Every man and woman in Britain was involved in the war effort in one way or another. Use books and the information from the television programme to explain what these people did to help the war effort.

munitions worker

fire worker

sailor

land girl

billeting officer

soldier

RAF pilot

APR warden

fireman

member of the Home Guard

Which job would you have chosen? Explain why.

Never Again

Aims

This documentary takes the story up to 1951 and the Festival of Britain. It looks at the aftermath of the war, and the development of the Welfare State.

Programme outline

Despite the VE Day celebrations, the end of the war was a time of austerity. But change was in the air.

Ken revisits Hollins Hall, the big house in the country where he was evacuated during the war and remembers the discrimination which he and his family faced. The experience made a permanent impression on him. He grew up opposed to privilege and determined to build a better and fairer society for all.

There were many who felt the same way and through Ken and Dorothy's memories we explore the post-war changes and their impact on everyday life. Contemporary footage is used to illustrate developments in housing, health care and education.

Background points

The Second World War changed the pattern of British life forever. It opened the nation's eyes to the poverty and deprivation endured by the poorest members of the community. Rationing and compulsory national service broke down class barriers and eroded the gap between the haves and have nots. It was clear that the country was unwilling to return to the poverty and inequity of the 1930s. The foundations of the Welfare State were laid during the war years and overwhelming support for the Labour party at the 1945 elections ensured that the work was continued during the first peace-time administration.

Time line

- 1944 The school leaving age is raised to fifteen
  All pupils are entitled to secondary education at a grammar, secondary modern or technical school
- 1945 Landslide victory for Labour at the first post-war elections
- 1946 Beginning of the 'New Towns' building programme
- 1948 Start of the National Health Service
- 1951 The Festival of Britain
- 1954 Rationing ends

Before viewing

Prepare the children to look out for:

- ways in which life changed after the war
- contrasts between then and now

Key words

anniversary, skivvy, polling day, prefab, National Health Service, VE Day (Victory in Europe Day), Winston Churchill, Battle of Britain, spitfires, Festival of Britain

After viewing

Recap and consolidation

- Why did the end of the war bring so many changes?
- What effect did they have on everyday life? Was it better to grow up before, or after the Second World War?
- Which of the changes discussed in the programme do children feel was the most important? Why?

Local investigation

After the war

Activity sheet 9 (page 22)

Look for clues to the changes that have taken place in your own area during, or immediately after the war.

Check war memorials and church records for information about casualties.

Look at the local secondary school. Many were built immediately after the war as a result of the 1944 Education Act. Primary schools were often extended or rebuilt to accommodate the post-war baby boom and evidence of alterations, or signs of the building's original function as an elementary school, may still remain.

Study aerial photographs and OS maps for evidence of post-war development. Look for housing estates, major roads, and public buildings such as libraries, hospitals and surgeries.

Take photographs of buildings from Victorian times, buildings from the 1950s and modern ones. Ask children to sort them into different categories. When they have got their eye in, take them for a walk round the local area and see if they can distinguish between different periods.

Get them to focus on one particular house, using Activity sheet 9 (page 22).

Changing town

Activity sheet 10 (page 23)

This activity could be followed up by a similar exercise based on the area around your school.

Class museum

Send out a letter home to parents asking for old household objects to start a class museum. Trawl friends and family as well to produce a small handling collection. Objects don't have to date from the period studied. In fact the wider the range, the better.

Begin with a period of exploration to help children to look closely at each object. These activities help to focus their attention.

Lucky dip. Wrap objects in a bag or scarf. Ask one child to put a hand in the bag and describe what the object feels like. Other children must try and guess what it is.

Mystery drawing. A pair of children sit back to back. One holds an object which it describes to the partner, who has to draw it from the description.

When children are familiar with the objects, turn them into museum curators. Their task is to sort the artefacts and put them in the right section of the museum. Broad categories, such as Before the War and After the War are best to begin with. Narrower distinctions, such as Victorian, very recent and wartime can be introduced if children prove successful. It is a good idea to include some material which can be easily dated, such as ration books, stamps or coins.

Encourage children to justify their sorting. 'I think this dates from the 1930s because...'

I think this comes from the 1960s because of the material and the zip. On the outside is net with normal material underneath

This dress is definitely from the 1920s because of the style and material

Scrap book

Complete the scrap book with a section on post-war life. Collect landmark events from local and family history as well as those of national significance. Family photographs could be photocopied and captioned. Children could look in local history books for pictures of the area in the fifties to be included in the scrap book. This kind of activity makes history relevant and helps children to understand their own place in the pattern.

Health checks

Children tend to think of health care in terms of treatment for illnesses or accidents. But the National Health Service had, and still has an important part to play in preventive medicine.

Ask children to talk about recent contacts with health care professionals. Who has been to the dentist, or the optician this term? Has anyone been immunised against flu or tetanus? Has the community nurse visited the school recently?

Talk about different categories of health care and use them as the basis of a class, or school survey.

This is how our class has used the National Health Service in the last term.

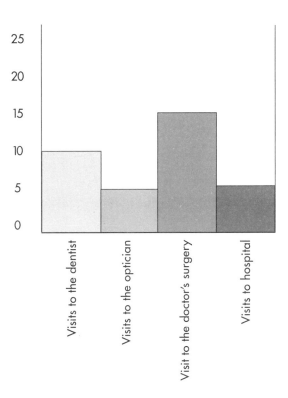

Houses

Address of house _____

Detached, semi detached, terraced, flat, bungalow other _____

How many windows can you see?

ground floor _____ first floor _____ second or other floors _____

Is there a chimney? _____

What is the house made of?_____

What do the walls look like? Draw the pattern they make here _____

Can you see any changes which have been made? _____

Are there any other special things you have noticed?_____

When do you think the house was built:

More than 100 years ago?   Less than 100 years ago?   Since the war?

Why do you think so?_____

Make a careful sketch of the house on the back of this sheet.

     How We Used to Live Britons at War

4 SCHOOLS

Changing Town

This map shows part of Rickton just before the war.

This map shows the same part of Rickton in the 1950s.

Find all the buildings which were built after the war. Colour them in on the second map.

Can you think why the new buildings have been built?

Which three named buildings have not changed?

Life in wartime Britain

Think of some of the special features of life in the war. Here are three to start you off. Find some more.

The blackout   Rationing   The Blitz

Draw lines between the features which go together and explain why they are linked.

How We Used to Live Britons at War

The quartermaster's stores

This song was very popular during the war. The quartermaster was the man who was in charge of food for soldiers.

There was bread, bread, as hard as lumps of lead
In the stores, in the stores
There was bread, bread, as hard as lumps of lead
In the quartermaster's stores

My eyes are dim, I cannot see
I have not brought my specs with me
I have not brought my specs with me

There was gravy, gravy, enough to float a navy
In the stores, in the stores
There was gravy, gravy, enough to float a navy
In the quartermaster's stores

My eyes are dim, I cannot see... etc

There was eggs, eggs, with great big hairy legs
In the stores, in the stores
There was eggs, eggs, with great big hairy legs
In the quartermaster's stores

My eyes are dim, I cannot see... etc

There was rats, rats, as big as blinking cats
In the stores, in the stores
There was rats, rats, as big as blinking cats
In the quartermaster's stores

My eyes are dim, I cannot see... etc

There were buns, buns, like bullets for the guns
In the stores, in the stores
There were buns, buns, like bullets for the guns
In the quartermaster's stores

My eyes are dim, I cannot see etc

▶ Draw a picture of your favourite verse.

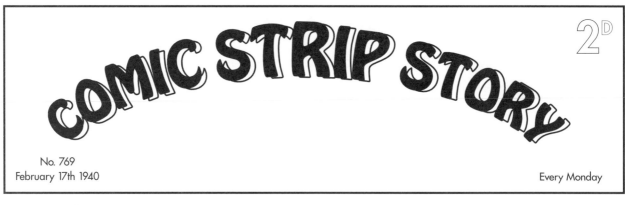

Make up a comic strip story about the evacuees and their adventures.

   How We Used to Live Britons at War

4 SCHOOLS

Documents

Everybody had to carry an identity card to show who they were.

This is what they looked like on the outside.

GK426478

1. **Always carry your Identity Card.**

2. **You are responsible for this Card, and must not part with it to any other person.**

3. **If you find a lost Identity Card you must hand it in at once at a Police Station.**

4. **Any breach of these requirements is an offence punishable by a fine or imprisonment or both.**

NATIONAL REGISTRATION

IDENTITY CARD

What kind of information might go on the inside?

Design the inside of your own identity card.

Places to visit

Scotland

The People's Palace, Glasgow Green, Glasgow, Scotland G40 1AT (0141 5540223)

Summerlee Heritage Trust, West Canal Street, Coatbridge, Lanarkshire (01236 431261)

The People's Story, Canongate Tolbooth, 163 Canongate, Edinburgh EH8 8BN (0131 5294057)

North East

Abbey House Museum, Kirkstall, Leeds LS5 3GH (01532 755821)

The Eden Camp Modern History Theme Museum, Malton, N. Yorks (01653 694444)

Lotherton Hall, Aberford, Leeds LS25 3EB (0113 2813259)

Newcastle Discovery, Blandford Square, Newcastle (0191 2326789)

Royal Armouries Museum, The Waterfront, Leeds, West Yorkshire LS10 1LT (0113 220 1888)

Dewsbury Museum Crow Nest Park, Heckmondwike Road, Dewsbury, West Yorkshire WF13 2SA (01924 468171)

North West

The Museum of Science and Industry in Manchester, Liverpool Road, Castlefield, Manchester M34 FP (0161 8330027)

Manchester Jewish Museum, 190 Cheetham Hill Road, Manchester M8 8LW (0161 834 9879). Early booking essential.

Lancashire County Museum, Stanley Street, Preston PR1 4YP (01772 264062 or 01772 254868)

Western Approaches, Rumford Street, Liverpool 2 (0151 2272008)

Midlands

The Tudor House Museum, Friar Street, Worcester WR1 2NA (01905 722349)

The Aerospace Museum, Cosford, Shifnal, Shropshire TF11 8UP (01902 374872)

Northampton Museum and Art Gallery, Guildhall Road, Northampton (01604 39415)

Birmingham Museum of Science and Industry, Newhall Street, Birmingham B3 (0121 2351661)

Coventry Cathedral, 7 Priory Row, Coventry, West Midlands (01203 227597)

East

Duxford Air Museum, Duxford Airfield, Cambridge CB2 4QR (01223 835000)

Seething Airfield Control Tower (US Air Force squadron) (01508 494850)

Muckleburgh Collection, Weybourne, Norfolk (01263 588210)

Lowestoft War Memorial Museum (01502 517950)

The Royal Naval Patrol Service Museum, Lowestoft (01502 586250)

South East

The Battle of Britain Museum, Hawkinge, Near Folkestone, Kent (01303 89 3140)

Biggin Hill Airfield, Kent (01959 571111)

The White Cliffs Experience, Market Place, Dover (01304 214566)

D-Day Museum, Clarence Esplanade, Southsea, Hampshire PO5 3NT (01705 827261)

Dover Castle and **Hellfire Corner** (01304 225229)

Tangmere Military Aviation Museum, Chichester, Sussex (01243 775223)

South West

The Packaging Museum, Llanthony Warehouse, The Docks, Gloucester, GL1 2EH (01452 307009)

Fleet Air Arm Museum, Yeovil, Somerset (01935 840565)

Swindon Museum, Bath Road, Swindon, Wilts SN1 4BA (01793 493188)

London

The Imperial War Museum, Lambeth Road, London SE1 6HZ (0171 416 5000) also HMS Belfast (0171 4076434)

The Museum of London, London Wall, London (0171 6003699)

The Cabinet War Rooms, Clive Steps, King Charles Street, London SW1A 2AQ (0171 9306961)

RAF Museum, Graham Park Way, Hendon, London NW9 5LL (0181 205 2266)

Watford Museum, 194, High Street, Watford, Herts (01923 232297)

Wales

The Museum of Welsh Life, St Fagans, Nr Cardiff (01222 569441)

Welsh Industrial & Maritime Museum, Cardiff (01222 481919)

Slate Museum, Llanberis (01286 870630)

Penrhos Cottage, c/o Scolton House & Museum, Spittle, Haverfordwest SA62 5QL (01437 731328)

Caernarfon Air Museum, Gwynedd (01286 830800)

Channel Islands

German Occupation Museum, Forest, Guernsey, Channel Islands (01481 38205)

Northern Ireland

Ulster Folk and Transport Museum, Witham Street Gallery, Belfast BT4 1HP (01232 451519)

Ulster Folk and Transport Museum, Cultra, Holywood NI BT18 0EU (01232 428428)